Crowd-Funding Explosion

How to raise money & beat the system!

By
Richard Encarnacion

Chapter 1

Ideas

The idea, many folks; I watched over the years, through online or had a personal conversation with, mentioned to me, that the idea was the hardest part. A solid idea, which can translate into a product, movie, new device, book or drawing.

Many folks believe, that the idea in itself, it's all, but it's not, the idea is a great starting point. That with passion, you can keep working to create something magical.

I read hundreds of book on success, literature, drawing, business and other topics, but I can frankly say, that idea are like the seed capital.

The fuel or money to begin working on the real idea.

For example: If your starting a business, you want to write, a business plan first, so your chances are better that you can open it and run it once, you select the business you want to open.

Because selecting a type of business is just selection, is not an idea.

But once you raise capital, let's say $100,000 and you make that business successful.

Then your running an idea, because if your idea was bad, you could of gone bankrupt, running the business and lost the money etc.

But if it's a good idea you can produce it, a great idea produces results. So it's vital that you follow this tips below, before embarking on an idea.

Make sure of the following:

1. You're extremely passionate about this topic, you can't sleep at night. (Not just how much money, but a project you love, that other can benefit, which can make money).

2. Do you have resources to get it off the ground? even if no one helps you or supports you?

You don't care what other people think, your so consumed, with this project, you want to get it done.

3. Even if everyone turns against you, you'll keep going? Or are you going to quit?

Are you prepared for risk, how you handle set back or risk?

Chapter 2

What you good at?

It's a common problem in today society, to find extremely
gifted people, living unsatisfied lives.

Sometimes people have to make hard choices, quit school and
get a job to support a family, if they have kid's at an early age.
Other times people had medical problems, problems from
war, the list is long.

In this chapter, I want to help you identify, areas that you that
your good at, to show you a small path or approach to take,
based on the example I will provide.

Yes, some extremely lucky, fortunate few are born gifted from
birth the other 7 Billion on the planet are not? Let's see.

The Directors Steven Spielberg, one of the most commercially successful directors in the film said, that if not for work, passion, dream, he would of never been able not only to compete with other equally brilliant directors, but how do you separate yourself from them.

Let's say you are Steven Spielberg, and you are working at a museum, as a security guard, or a Janitor or maybe even at a train station.

Now your thinking Rick, you're going nuts right, come on. How can someone like Steven Spielberg, work at a place like that? Think about it, theirs thousands of people in the world like him, with different skills who are working at jobs they hate, everyday; because they have to support their families.

But is that the best use of his talent? Of course not.

Is your gift being used? Steven Spielberg gift is film-making. Would it be beneficial to Steven Spielberg, to have become something other than a Director? Probably not, because he probably would have not been as good at it. If he could make money? Let's say his an unknown, can he make money today? No.

But can he make money after a couple of years, and he shows his work and people know what he can do? yep.

Maybe it would not have been beneficial for him to have become an engineer, No right. Just because the money is great, doesn't mean you'll be great at it. Or that you would enjoy what your doing.

So even thought Steven Spielberg, would have to start as a movie extra, today if he wasn't a known Hollywood director. Could he eventually be in a position, he would like, if he worked hard at what he loved? Yes, absolutely.

Theirs people who are mechanics, and are great artist, construction workers who are musicians, painters who work in factories, you don't have to quit your day job. But find out, what are you amazing at? Because, maybe that is what your missing.

An easy way for you to discover, what you're good or talented at, is begin showing people samples, especially if your nervous about showing your work.
Begin doing music once a week, art the following week, photography the next and so on. Until you discover your hidden talent.

Then show people, you also look at it, hear it, smell it if it's cooking your talent lol, taste it if you can :).

what do you find? What is your talent? Do you love it?

The examples below, will help to identify different areas; that can help you narrow it down to a few.

1. What would a stranger pay you for? If they saw, herd it or smelled it?

2. How easy or difficult is if for you to do it?

3. How much time does it take?

Where can you do it? Garage? Closet? bedroom?Outside?

where can you produce work?

Chapter 3

Who you Re-present?

This chapter, really hit me hard, once I started thinking about it, because the topic is so obvious and you might say wow, he doesn't know this or why was it so hard for him? But once you begin to think about it, you become a doubtful as I was, I mean.

I'm a pretty confident guy, I was a former Marine, Can't get more confident than that.

But the topic of who you represent, really delves much deeper

that that, who we think we are, how well adjusted we are. Our

families, etc.

In this topic, the conversation of who you represent; I am

making a statement. An I am speaking in terms, of what

others view me. Not how I view myself, because I could have

a great way of looking at myself, but if others don't see me as

someone, in the same way I see myself, it's kind of pointless.

Do I come across to others as controlling ? Manipulative?

Passionate? Relaxed? Humorist? Goofy?

This has more to do with external perceptions, than internal,

as I grew up in the east coast.

I think growing up in big cities, like New York, Miami, New Jersey, Los Angeles, Boston, Dallas, you learn more about social mechanics, than if I grew up in the country.

Because if you grew up in a city, you can obviously say it's different than growing up in the country side. In the country side, people are more relaxed, trustful and straight forward, honest and usually down to earth people, with a friendly demeanor. Am not saying people are not this in the city, but is more prevalent in the country side.

Since I grew up in the city, I noticed that people put barriers, facades, faces, clothes to hide themselves.

As you communicate with people, and people learn more about you, the goals or intentions, which you carry with you.

It becomes clear for people, to make a distinction of who you are.

If you were to show two distinct people, to be seen by a crowd. An you bring in someone wearing a suit, and another person wearing baggy jeans and a t-shirt. People are going to have two different perceptions, about this people, unless their celebrities. It can be the same person, and wearing two different sets of clothes; you will get two distinct opinions.

Who do you think, would be perceived as more Educated?

More successful? Who has a better job?

Suit right! OR is that what you would think.

Let's say communication, use of words, slang; if you was

going to communicate with a business person and every other

word or topic. Was a slang, what impression you think would

that person have of you? Would it be professional? No, right.

As you go out into the real world, and communicate, we are

viewed a certain way, and sometimes, we are uncomfortable

with that perception.

So look at yourself, in the mirror once a week. And Say:

What Image, Am I representing?

⅄ Do my clothes?

*My grooming?

⅄ My speech ?

⅄ My Smile?

⅄ Tell a story of who I am?

⅄ Am I viewed the way I want to be viewed?

Chapter 4

Do I view the world, in an interesting way?

Theirs not many people, who view the world, with an open

mind for ideas and creative exploration; for something

completely different, from what is already on this earth, But

those who do, enjoy the many benefits that it gives.

One of my favorite authors, is something I call an Explorer.

Her name is J.K. Rowling, you know her story. She is the

mega famous writer, who wrote Harry Potter Series. Her ideas

are universally known, so well known. That they beat the

bible in sales for a couple of years. Her stories are read by

children and adults from around the globe. Through many

languages, and versions.

It began several years ago, after she had her daughter. She was a school teacher, who recently was separated from her husband, and had moved back to the U.K. While she was on a train everyday, a story caught her imagination. An she began to write a story, which took her five years to complete. Everyday, she would do the same on the train, seat her young daughter and begin writing.

She had encountered many setbacks, and problems before she began, along the way, one of these problems was that she was on government support. This issue by itself, would have stopped the majority of people and would have been seen as a major obstacle, she was a single mother, raising her kid on her own.

Her imaginative mind, an her view of the world proved to be unique, because in the years in which her book became published, children book sales was at an all time low, and the internet was taking over.

Even thought she faced all these obstacles, all these incredible odds, her book seemed to be at a loss, and the industry moving away.

She became incredibly successful. Her books, toys and movies are known to every kid across the world, and because of this her life is forever changed and so as the people who read, watch, see her stories.

Chapter 5
Always do projects.

Recently, I was attending a class for Digital Production. An during the class one of the unique, things which actually got my attention, was how many different people; we had in class who had come from different backgrounds, experiences, education, an it really got me excited; because I learned. That two of my classmates were mini- celebrities.

One of my classmates had just become a professional skateboarder. An the other had a YouTube channel with over 100,000 views on each of his small three minute shows.

During the class, the teacher had asked us to share our experience, work background, education, especially what has gotten us to were we are today. To say I was stunned, is a little bit toned.

What my classmates, both said in their own words was that their status, was as a result of their projects, they never made major projects.

But they always made projects, one of the guys had made over 20 projects, on video, over the course of two years.

Which is about one project every 2 months or so, the other said he skated everyday and he post projects on the web, with his phone or iPad.

The surprising piece of information came to me as a result of questions, the first was did you intended to become an e-celebrity.

He said No. He just had a passion for the Digital video project and was so successful at it, that he was being recognized as an expert in his field.

The other said yes, that it was his life long goal, but after he left for Iraq. He forgot, as soon as he made it back; he got into it again and stumbled into pro skating.

I was surprised and kinda shocked, both times, their answer threw me off completely. As I had always, herd from successful people that you need to have a plan, be able to follow through. Put in hard work and know the results.

For the next couple of days, I Stayed plugged in. I was listening actively to all conversations they had, one thing started happening, in my own personal life, which I haven't done in a long time. Which is that, I began making projects, doing little 30 second projects, one minute shoots.

Soon, I was taking their advise, making small crappy projects; putting them on YouTube; Facebook and other social media sites.

One ingredient, I was missing was passion, So I started
working on projects, I would be passionate about only.
Something funny started happening.

On the projects, I didn't care about I got 2-3 views, on the
projects that I was passionate about I got 1,300 views on
Vimeo. Which is a hard site to get any attention on.

That is just one example, of what you need to do; in order to
work your plan, and have a passion to get your goal.

An most importantly make something out of it. Get' er done.

Chapter 6

Crowd funding

The meat and potatoes, yep. Along with the internet, laptop, computers, netflix, portable tooth brushes, and instant food, crowd funding is one of the best inventions of the 21st and 22nd century in my book.

The alternative to crowd funding is a monster, something so scary I don't like thinking about it. Many people have got nightmares at night, some people even call it the buggy man lol. Well the alternative is Hollywood or big investors, who sometimes don't see the potentials of small indie projects, the same way in which a small artist might see a project.

Some of the ideas that have been funded through social media sites, such as indiegogo, and kick-starter. Like ideas and dreams. The projects for which might have never seen the light of day, this site has seen the rise and fall of some ideas. Giving the opportunity for self expression and open community to foster talent and creativity.

It has changed how artist, investors, designers, engineers, and writers of people view the world. An the possibilities, I see it too.

The two major sites, Kick-starter & Indiegogo.

Have raised, awareness of projects, gained exposure for themselves, and helped people raise millions of dollars all while following a system designed to help anyone and giving something of value in return.

Some of the projects that have gained attention, as well as received funding range from film, games, design, books all of which have received millions of dollars in funding.

During my research, for the documentary I produced, called

anti-Hollywood, I Learned that their are important steps that

have to be taken into consideration, for a successful campaign.

Either on a social media, or indie to-go or kick starter.

10 Steps for a successful Campaign

1. Have a group of friends or a following.

2. Create a professional video presentation.

3. Offer hits & incentives.

4. Have a personal site for project.

5. Use social Media to advertise.

6. Use blog to market project.

7. Prepare a script for a video of what to say.

8. Building steps of project.

9. Building the campaign page

10. Evidence that you can develop the project and have the ability to develop it.

Resources:

kickstarter.com/help/school#setting_your_goal
www.indiegogo.com
http://www.happymittengames.com/do-your-research-before-using-kickstarter/
http://www.fourhourworkweek.com/blog/2012/12/18/hacking-kickstarter-how-to-raise-100000-in-10-days-includes-successful-templates-e-mails-etc/
http://launchandrelease.com/what-to-expect-when-launching-a-kickstarter/

My site
www.behance.com/richardencarnacion
https://vimeo.com/72239925_ - Anti-Hollywood documentary.
https://vimeo.com/62919355 – the video with 1,350 views I mentioned.

Tip:

Also be sure to check out **kick starter school**.